BLACKBEARD
THE FIERCEST PIRATE OF ALL

BLACKBEARD

THE
FIERCEST PIRATE
OF ALL

By NORMAN C. PENDERED

Times Printing Company, Inc.
Manteo, North Carolina

Library of Congress Catalog Card Number: 75-5323

Second Printing, 1983

To Peg and Tom Haigwood
who first aroused my interest in Blackbeard
in the fall of 1969
when they invited me to the pirate country
of North Carolina.

PROLOGUE

It was into a world of unsettled conditions, including hard times, war, pestilence, privateering, and piracy, that Blackbeard was born and grew into manhood. For many long years England had been at war; the war of the Spanish Succession lasted from 1702 to 1713. During this time her privateers played an important role in the struggle. Following the Peace of Utrecht many of her unemployed seamen, especially privateers, created the greatest era of piracy the world has ever known.

It is truly written that war makes privateers and peace hangs them. Blackbeard was both privateer and pirate, but he probably gave little or no thought to the distinction between the two. However, there have always been clearly defined differences.

Privateering was a business enterprise wherein armed, privately-owned vessels of one nation captured vessels, particularly merchantmen, of another nation when a state of war existed between the two nations. Three important features characterize privateering: (1) a state of war must exist between the two nations involved, (2) the privateer must carry a commission or letter of marque issued by the government whose flag she flies, and (3) only vessels of the enemy nation may be taken.

On the other hand, piracy is deliberate robbery or violence on the high seas or an attack from the sea against a coastal community for the personal gain of the attackers who do not hold a commission (letter of marque) from an established government.

When Blackbeard became a pirate he became an international outlaw and was subject to extermination or seizure and trial by the designated court of any country whether or not he victimized their ships or nationals. The reason for this is that piracy is considered to be a crime not against one nation but against all mankind and therefore pirates are regarded as the enemies of the human race (hostis humani generis).

Economic conditions in Blackbeard's times were extremely favorable for the rise and growth of piracy. Spain, France, and England had laws which forbade their colonists to trade directly with foreigners. Each insisted that their colonists trade exclusively with or through the mother country. Manufactured goods and luxury items were generally in short supply throughout the New World. To meet this need there arose a smuggling trade which flowered into piracy. One of the important requisites for piracy is a market to dispose of plunder. Unless pirates can find receivers for their stolen goods, they cannot make a profit. Markets for pirates' goods existed aplenty in the New World. Most colonists were eager to buy goods cheaply; they did not ask the smuggler or the pirate where he got his goods so long as the exchange was fair either in gold or by barter.

Geographically, Blackbeard lived in a setting which was very favorable to piratical activities. A pirate needs isolated lurking places in relatively shoal waters so he cannot be pursued by warships and so he can hide out between raids without danger of being seized. At the same time these spots need to be close to shipping lanes where richly loaded merchantmen sail. In short, a pirate needs a lurking place in which to hide and from which he can strike suddenly and as quickly disappear. Blackbeard's world, especially the West Indies, met all of these geographic requirements and was indeed an ideal environment for piracy to flourish.

Thus it was that Blackbeard lived in an age that embodied the three elements necessary for the rise of piracy. These are (1) *men* who are willing to risk their lives as pirates for the rewards of stolen plunder, (2) *markets* for pirates' goods, and (3) *bases* from which pirates can strike. Under these conditions it is small wonder that a man of Blackbeard's nature and character chose not the dull life of an ordinary seaman, but followed the call of gold, battle, and the adventure of piracy on the high seas!

BLACKBEARD

THE FIERCEST PIRATE OF ALL

Will you hear of a bloody Battle,
Lately fought upon the Seas,
It will make your Ears to rattle,
And your Admiration cease;
Have you heard of Teach the Rover,
And his Knavery on the Main;
How of Gold he was a Lover,
How he lov'd all ill got Gain.

— *Benjamin Franklin*

The golden age of piracy in the New World reached its zenith during the early 1700's. Of all the pirates active during this period, the name of Blackbeard stands out. Although his career as a pirate was short-lived, lasting only 27 months, in that brief time Blackbeard earned immortality in the annals of crime as one of the most ferocious pirate kings of all time. If not the most diabolic villain the New World ever spawned, certainly Blackbeard ranks among the top few. He is considered by many as the ''fiercest pirate of them all.''

Most writers on the subject report that Blackbeard was born in Bristol, England, but whether this is true or not is most uncertain. It is also said that he was the illegitimate child of a barmaid and a nobleman, but this too is sheer conjecture. The truth is that there is no known record of his parentage nor of his early life. Nothing is known of his schooling, if indeed, he ever went to school. His very name is shrouded in mystery. Colonial papers refer to him as Captain Edward Teach, Thach, Tach, Tache, Tatch, Teatch, or Thatch. Lieutenant Maynard, the young King's officer who ended Blackbeard's career in bloody hand-to-hand battle, referred to him as Captain Teach and this name has been commonly accepted since that time.

Teach, Tache, Thatch, or whatever, this Colonial gangster achieved infamy as Blackbeard the pirate. Evidence from early records indicates that he was a ruffian and a scoundrel with a quick, violent temper and a generally nasty disposition. Like all outlaws, he took by force the material possessions of others with contempt showing on his face and in his heart. Without hesitation he would betray associates and even long-time friends; he was loyal to no man save himself.

Wherever Blackbeard went ''a-pyrating'' he left frightened men and screaming women and children in his wake. Mere mention of his name would strike immediate terror in the hearts of stout colonists, sailors, merchant captains, and even royal Governors from the West Indies to New England. Many a ship's captain surrendered without resistance when he learned that the approaching ship flying the skull and crossbones at her masthead was commanded by none other than the fearsome Blackbeard himself. At the siege of Charles Town (Charleston, S.C.) horror-stricken citizens stampeded through the streets in sheer panic when it became known that Blackbeard was off the bar and threatened to attack the town with his ship's cannon. For more reasons than one, this brute of a man ''frightened America more than any Comet that has appeared there in a long time (1 : p. 33).

Blackbeard believed in hurting or frightening nearly every individual with whom he came in contact. Not only did he believe it, he practiced it religiously! One of the legends about this pirate chief is that he fell in love with a beautiful girl who spurned his love for that of a handsome seaman. She gave the young man her ring to show her love for him was true. Unfortunately, the ship on which the seaman sailed was taken by Blackbeard who immediately recognized his rival. He cut off the man's left hand — the one containing the girl's ring — placed it in an ornate silver casket and sent it off to the young lady. Upon opening the silver box, the girl swooned in dead faint and shortly afterwards died of a broken heart.

On another occasion Blackbeard was drinking heavily in his cabin with three men including his Sailing Master, Israel Hands, and the ship's pilot.

Without any provocation whatever Blackbeard sneakily slipped two of his pistols from their holsters and cocked them under the table. Neither Hands nor the pilot seemed to notice Blackbeard's actions, but the third man did and quickly left the room to go on deck. The pirate chief blew out the candle and crossing his hands underneath the table, discharged both pistols at his men. One of the balls did no damage, but the other struck Israel Hands in the knee and crippled him for life.

Later the Quarter Master said, "Captain, why did ye do such a thing to your men?"

Blackbeard swore loudly and growled, "If I do not kill one of ye now and then, ye'll forget who I am!"

The fear image created by Blackbeard resulted not only from his piratical atrocities, but from his satanic looks as well. Early in his career he discovered that a grisly appearance completely unnerved his victims. For this reason Blackbeard always made special efforts to look like and act like the Devil incarnate. Sketches and drawings (see Figures 1 & 2) picture him with dense black hair covering his face up to his eyes and stretching downward to his waist. It is said that he twisted the hair near his ears into small loops. In time of battle he stuck "lighted matches" into these loops and under his hat so as to illuminate his face with an unearthly glow. The smoke and fire from these slow-

Figure 1
Blackbeard, the fiercest pirate of all.

Figure 2
The mighty Blackbeard and his crew ready for combat.

burning matches together with his wild, black, piercing eyes and the six pistols slung in a bandolier over his hairy chest made him a dreadful and terrible sight to behold. Even the very air about him seemed tinged with fumes of fiery brimstone straight from the pits of hell. Figure 2 depicts Blackbeard ready for battle.

It is believed that Edward Teach, the great Blackbeard, began his infamous career of piracy during the late summer or fall of the year 1716. Prior to this time he is thought to have shipped aboard privateers out of Jamaica during Queen Anne's War (1702-1713). He received his early training in the fine art of piracy from an expert, that veteran pirate Captain Benjamin Hornigold. Apparently Hornigold saw in this swaggering bully a man who was naturally endowed with great talent for robbing others on the high seas. Teach proved to be an apt pupil and quickly learned his trade both from Hornigold and from the other rogues who put in at New Providence (Nassau) in the Bahama Islands. The best and the worst of the pirate lot in the New World had set up a huge stronghold at New Providence and it is said that nearly 2000 pirates were gathered there (see chart, Figure 3, pages 20-21).

One day upon capturing a sloop, Hornigold sent Teach aboard in charge of the prize crew. Hornigold and Teach now sailed in consort. The reason for this was simply that in those days pirates liked to "go on the account" in pairs which made it easier for them to stalk and capture their prey. Hornigold and Teach continued this mutually-satisfactory arrangement until just before Hornigold repented his life of sin and accepted the King's mercy in accordance with his Majesty's proclamation to pardon all pirates who surrendered.

Sailing from New Providence to the North American coast in the spring of 1717, Teach and Hornigold ransacked a number of ships along the way. Among these vessels was a small one from Havana carrying 120 barrels of flour. They also took a sloop from Bermuda under the command of Captain Thurbar. After removing his cargo of wine, they let Thurbar and his vessel proceed otherwise unmolested. As the pirates neared the coastline, they captured a vessel bound from Maderia to South Carolina. The plunder taken here was added to the stolen goods already in the pirates' booty.

On reaching the Virginia coast, the pirates anchored in a secluded cove to careen their ships. They knew that a pirate vessel must be a fast sailer and careening was necessary a couple of times a year to remove barnacles from the ship's sides and bottom. It was tough, back-breaking work for all but the pirates accepted it as a necessary evil. First the crew waited until high tide when they brought each ship as close as possible to the shore. As the tide slackened all hands heaved the vessel over on her side by means of block and tackle whose lines were attached to solid footings ashore, usually stout trees. While the tide was low, the men worked feverishly to clean and tallow the exposed side and half the bottom of the vessel. After this laborious task was completed, the exhausted men righted the ship on an incoming tide. The process of scraping, cleaning, and tallowing the other side was repeated as before. Every pirate from the Captain to the cabin boy knew that careening was a dangerous operation because with their ship aground, they were virtually at the mercy of any enemy vessel which sighted them and moved in for the kill. The need for haste was evident to all, so every pirate worked like fury and was urged on by the merciless goading of their pirate leaders.

The cleaned pirate ships now headed back toward the West Indies. Somewhere off the Bahamas, near the 24th latitude, they captured a large vessel from French Guinea sailing for Martinique. Hornigold permitted Teach to become master of the guineaman. This was a turning point in Teach's career for this vessel was to become his pirate flagship. Descriptive details on the vessel have been lost in antiquity. It is likely, however, that she was a two-decker, perhaps 100 feet long with a beam of 20 feet, and square rigged.

About this time Teach, now Captain Teach, and Captain Hornigold went their separate ways, but they always remained compatriots and confederates. Sometime later Hornigold sailed to New Providence to await the arrival of Captain Woodes Rogers, the newly-appointed Governor, in order to surrender to mercy, pursuant to the King's Proclamation. He had a rather long wait because Governor Rogers did not arrive at Nassau until July 26, 1718.

Eager to prove himself as a pirate leader and arrogantly confident of his ability, Teach mounted 40 guns aboard the newly-captured French Guineaman and renamed her the *Queen Anne's Revenge.* In those days pirates were wont to rechristen captured vessels with new names often involving the word *revenge.* There was even one pirate ship called the *Revenge's Revenge.*

To keep his post as the captain of a pirate ship, Teach knew that he must control his officers and crew. He accomplished this by making them fear him and by ruling them with an iron fist. He never hesitated to "lay the cat" on the back of an unruly crew member. The pirate chief realized that his men were a tough lot, but that he had to be tougher. If they were strong, he had to be stronger; if they were brave, he had to be braver. In other words, he had to excel in everything the pirate band did.

One day at sea when no prey was in sight and being a little full with drink, Blackbeard said to his crew, "Come, let us make a Hell of our own, and try how long we can bear it" (1: p. 33). Then he and several others went below into the ship's hold. After closing up all the hatches, they filled several pots with brimstone and other combustible matter and set them on fire. The hold rapidly filled with sulphurous fumes and soon the men were coughing, choking, spitting, and gasping for air. All of the men, save Teach, quickly sprang for the ladder and tumbled up to the fresh air on the deck. When Blackbeard finally left the hold and arrived topsides, he swore vehemently, "Damn ye," he exclaimed, "ye yellow _____ _____ _____!" Spatting on the deck and shaking his fist at them he snarled, "I'm a better man than all ye milksops put together."

Cruising off the island of St. Vincent, Teach and his men took the *Great Allen*, a large ship under the command of Captain Christopher Taylor. The pirates ravaged her cargo, put the captured crew ashore on St. Vincent's Island, and then burned the *Great Allen* to her waterline.

Flushed with his success against the *Great Allen*, Teach never hesitated to engage the next vessel he sighted which happened to be the *HMS Scarborough*, a fifth-rate British man-of-war mounting 30 guns. Under the command of Captain Francis Hume and carrying 140 men, the *Scarborough* was returning to her duty station at Barbados. She was one of more than a dozen vessels ordered by his Majesty King George I to suppress piracy in the West Indies and along the North American coastline.

The pirate problem in the New World had rapidly reached huge proportions. Merchants, masters of ships, and passengers including several governors of the provinces had complained bitterly to his Majesty about the pirates. In response to this pressure the King had issued a special order at Whitehall on September 5, 1716. In this royal edict the King pointed out that pirates had grown so numerous near Jamaica and along the North American coast that trade from Great Britain to those areas was not only being obstructed, but in imminent danger of being lost. Thereupon the King had deployed a royal fleet to seek out and destroy the pirates. The fourteen ships comprising this naval force boasted a combined firepower of 336 guns. They were assigned duty stations at Jamaica, Barbados, the Leeward Islands, Virginia, New York, and New England.

It is interesting to note that the hands of Death had slowly begun to close around Blackbeard's neck even at this early stage in his career. Some of the King's officers and men who were eventually to destroy him had already arrived in Virginia waters aboard two guardships of his Majesty's navy. The actors, scenery, and props were slowly assembling on the great stage of life. Only Time kept them waiting behind stage until the last grains of sand trickled through the hour glass to signal the beginning of the death scene of Edward Teach, master pirate. Soon enough officers and men selected from the King's ships, *Lyme* and *Pearl*, would be fighting to the death with Blackbeard and his pirate band with no quarter being given nor asked on either side.

Undisturbed by any premonition of his fate, Teach attacked the *HMS Scarborough* with full vigor. The running battle which ensued between the two vessels raged several hours, but with inconclusive results. Teach and his pirate crew must have fought fiercely against such a formidable foe as the *Scarborough* because English naval vessels of this period had fighting crews whose gunners were among the best in the world. His Majesty's officers and men must have fought well, too, for their 30 guns were ten less than those carried by the *Queen Anne's Revenge*.

Finally, both ships retired from the scene of battle. It is not clear why Captain Hume chose to retreat rather than to pursue the pirate foe to the bitter death. It is a matter of record, however, that the *Scarborough* had just buried 20 crewmen and 40 others were sick. For this reason she was ill equipped to go to sea — let alone pursue pirates. The outcome of this battle greatly augmented Blackbeard's conceit for he had won a draw with a mighty fighting ship of his Majesty's navy!

Perhaps the Captain of the *Scarborough* was prudent to withdraw from battle on this occasion. Pirates "on the account" were generally a blood-thirsty lot and wicked fighters who seldom gave quarter. Sometime later the *Scarborough* went out from her duty station in pursuit of a pirate vessel commanded by William Mudie. The pirates not only killed the *Scarborough's* Captain and some of his crew, but carried off his Majesty's ship as well.

English tradition had it that attack whom they might, English pirates always respected English ships. This was not really true, of course, but the idea had sentimental appeal to some of the King's subjects. Teach was probably English, but he was one of those pirates who disregarded sentimentality and tradition and sought to capture any and all ships, English or otherwise, that took his fancy. As noted, Captain Teach showed no respect for any vessel on the high seas, not even for his Majesty's man-of-war!

Blackbeard and his men now headed toward the Spanish Main, a name given by buccaneers and pirates to the northern coast of South America. It included the coastline of what is now Venezuela and Columbia. This area was originally called the Spanish Mainland because Spain controlled large portions of the mainland of South America as well as the West Indies and other islands in the Caribbean Sea. In common usage English seamen shortened the term to the Spanish Main.

Enroute to the Main, Teach came upon another pirate vessel, the *Revenge*. She was a 12-gun sloop manned by 70 pirates under the command of Captain Stede Bonnet. This chance meeting of the pirate captains was to affect greatly both of their lives in the months they had remaining to live.

Stede Bonnet was a storybook pirate come to life. He was the only pirate in history known to purchase a vessel in which to go a-pyrating. The "esteemed" Mr. Bonnet was only one of the very few pirates to make his victims walk the plank. Contrary to general opinion, such practice was rarely, if ever, used by pirates in the New World. There is evidence, however, that early pirates in the Red Sea area did employ this heartless form of execution, deriving from it an inordinate sense of pleasure. Bonnet proved himself unorthodox in other ways. One day after capturing a ship off Long Island (New York), he put his men ashore with cash to pay for certain provisions he needed. Indeed, Bonnet was a strange kind of pirate.

Stede Bonnet had retired from the British Army with the rank of Major. He had settled on the island of Barbados where he was regarded as a cultured, well educated gentleman and a plantation owner of some financial means. He was honored and respected by all on the island. Apparently one day he decided to become a pirate because of the adventuresome life it seemed to offer. Johnson writes that:

> "this Humour of going a pyrating, proceeded from a Disorder in his Mind, which had been but too visible in him, some Time before this wicked Undertaking; and which is said to have been occasioned by some Discomforts he found in a married state."
>
> (1: p. 36)

It is said that Bonnet took up piracy to escape the nagging tongue of his wife. Rumor had it that the evening he sailed from Barbados to begin pirating, he left his wife without even saying good-bye.

It did not take Blackbeard long to discover that Bonnet lacked practical experience in the ways of life at sea. He was weak in navigation and could not control his men. Worse yet, he suffered a deplorable lack in even the fundamentals of good piracy. Teach surmised that Bonnet was by nature a weak individual who was easily influenced; thereupon he invited Bonnet aboard the *Queen Anne's Revenge* where he craftily prevailed upon him to permit Lieutenant Richards to take command of the *Revenge.* Teach advanced the argument that a fine gentleman like the Major need not suffer the responsibilities, burdens, and uncertainties of pirating aboard his own vessel. Instead, he persuaded the Major that he deserved an easier life aboard a larger, more comfortable ship where the adventures and financial rewards of piracy would be as great. When Bonnet passively submitted, Teach knew that his character assessment was correct and from that day forward Teach dominated Bonnet wherever they sailed. Bonnet was virtually a prisoner aboard the pirate flagship until many months later when Blackbeard broke up his pirate company on the way northward following the siege of Charles Town. Despite what has just been stated about Bonnet's frailties as a man and a pirate, he proved in the end to be a pretty formidable pirate after all; in fact, the reward posted for his capture exceeded even that offered for the great Blackbeard.

Blackbeard did not need Major Stede Bonnet at all, but he could make use of his vessel and crew. As mentioned previously, pirates liked to ''go on the account'' in pairs which made it easier to stalk and capture their prey. And so it was that the *Queen Anne's Revenge* under Captain Teach together with Bonnet's sloop, the *Revenge*, under Lieutenant Richards, sailed in consort. They made first for Turneffe, an island off the coast of Guatemala which was not far from the Bay of Honduras.

Upon reaching Turneffe the pirate ships lay at anchor in the deep water harbor to take on fresh water and victuals. Meantime the men amused themselves in the little village which stretched between the shoreline and the surrounding hills. The town itself was nothing more than a cluster of miserable huts and disreputable shacks many of which were made from discarded sails. Filthy, noisy, wild, and full of violence, Turneffe lived up to its name as a popular pirate resort in the New World. Rum, whiskey, and grog flowed freely in all the huts and shacks.

Women were not allowed aboard a pirate vessel at sea. The penalty was death for any crewman who seduced a female aboard, even under disguise, and carried her to sea. Here at Turneffe things were different. Harlots, Jezebels, and jades were everywhere and each had her price. So long as a man's gold held out, he need never be lonely for a woman's company.

Gambling was a welcome diversion for the corsairs since it, too, was strictly taboo aboard a pirate vessel at sea. On the Turneffe beach gold exchanged hands quickly and easily to the soft shuffle of the cards and the click of the dice.

Since there was no place at sea to spend their ill-gotten loot, the pirates were determined to enjoy life fully whenever ashore. Turneffe provided them the opportunity they sought. Wine, women, and song were the order of the day and night reveling — so long as the pirate gold lasted! In their greed for drinking and gambling and in their lust for women, the men saw not the squalor nor the riotous, violent, sinful living; instead, they saw in Turneffe a pirate's paradise — a heaven on earth.

Leaving the Bay of Honduras in their wake, Blackbeard and his men set a course for Turkill. Later they sailed to Grand Caimaines which is a tiny island about ten miles west of Jamaica. Here they captured a small vessel engaged in turtling. This haul made a valuable contribution to the food larder. There was no refrigeration aboard ships in those days, so fresh vegetables, fruit, or meats would last only a few days. Turtles could be kept alive indefinitely on a ship with little or no attention and thus constituted a tasty and ready source of meat for use anytime.

After looting the turtler the pirate band journeyed to Havana. From here they sailed to the Bahama Wrecks where pirates and others liked to dive for treasure in the hulks of the sunken Spanish treasure ships.

Every year the great Spanish Plate fleet had sailed homeward loaded with a vast treasure in gold and silver from the New World. Spanish galleons collected the yearly hoard at key seaports, such as, Porto Bello, Cartagena, and Vera Cruz. Even from faraway Manila the Spaniards shipped gold bullion to Acapulco, Mexico where it was carried overland to Vera Cruz. The final rendezvous for the treasure fleet was Havana. From here the flotilla sailed with the Gulf Stream between Florida and the Bahamas

Figure 3 —

Blackbeard's hunting grounds in the West Indies.

and thence along the northern trade route to Spain (see Figure 3, pages 20-21).

In 1714 the Plate Fleet had been wiped out by a devastating hurricane and wrecked on the reef-ridden tip of Florida. For that year the treasure from the New World was totally lost. Since that time many seamen had found it profitable to "fish the Spanish wrecks" by diving in the shallow waters after pieces of eight. Some found it more profitable to steal the gold and silver pieces from those who had already reclaimed them and were still fishing there. At any rate such pastime was relaxing from the usual pirate activities.

Tired of diving for treasure, the pirate blackguards pushed on toward the Carolina coast. On the way they captured two sloops and a brigantine. Sometime during the summer (1717) perhaps on this voyage northward, the pirates lay off the bar at Charles Town and took two incoming vessels.

During his brief career as a pirate, Blackbeard's depredations were conducted over a vast hunting ground ranging from the Spanish Main to the Bay of Honduras and throughout the many islands of the Caribbean Sea as well as far up the North American coast (see Figure 3, pages 20-21). Two of his favorite retreats were Bath Town (Bath) and Ocacock, North Carolina (now Ocracoke Island on the Outer Banks). Ocacock Inlet was one of the three best inlets along the entire North Carolina coast and served Bath Town which was a principal port of entry at this time. This vast area contained innumerable bays, coves, and secluded spots in the Pamticoe Sound (now Pamlico), the Pamticoe River, and the Neuse River. The region was sparsely populated so that a pirate vessel might hide out for any length of time without undue observation from passersby. Figure 4 shows Blackbeard's haunts in the Carolina Province: Fishtown (now Beaufort), Topsail Inlet, Ocacock Inlet, Teach's Hole, Pamticoe Sound, and Bath Town.

The relationship between pirates and merchants was economic in nature. Gold and silver coins as well as general merchandise were in short supply in the towns and villages. This hampered trade and forced a kind of barter system on the people. Usually the pirates had plenty of coins and often valuable cargo from plundered ships. On the other hand the merchants had materials and supplies which the pirates needed. They also had plenty of drink and other forms of entertainment available. Thus, an exchange of mutual benefit took place. To salve their consciences, some merchants simply ''closed one eye'' in dealing with pirates while pretending that they knew not the source of the cargo or gold coin which the pirates had to exchange. Other merchants could care less where the goods came from so long as the price was right.

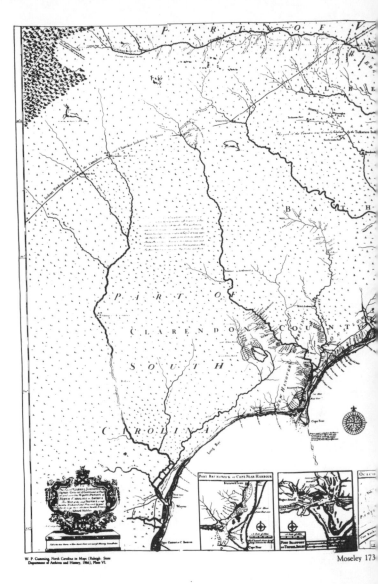

Moseley 173

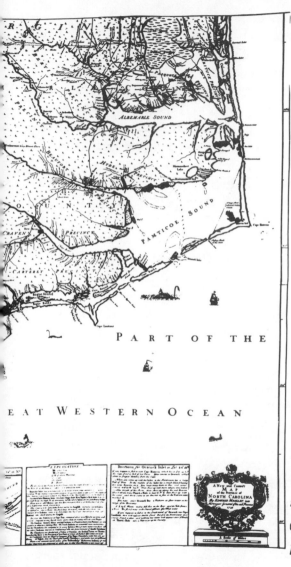

Figure 4 —

Blackbeard's

haunts

in the

Carolina

Province.

In January, 1718 Blackbeard and his pirate crew surrendered at Bath Town to Governor Eden of North Carolina under the terms of the proclamation of King George I for suppressing piracy in the New World. Although the period of amnesty was later extended, the initial date for granting mercy expired on January 5. The pirates received certificates of pardon from his Excellency the Governor.

It is not known exactly what Teach's motive in surrendering was, but doubtless, it was an ulterior one. Idle gossip of the times hinted that Governor Eden and his staff were hospitable to pirates. The arrangement between Blackbeard and Eden has never been uncovered, if indeed any such agreement actually existed. There is strong evidence to believe, however, that Governor Eden and Tobias Knight, the Secretary of North Carolina, granted certain favors to Blackbeard in return for pirate loot.

In throwing himself on the King's mercy, Blackbeard agreed to abandon forever the ways of piracy and to live henceforth an honest, upright life. His crew members scattered themselves throughout the plantations and provinces; some of them went to Virginia, Pennsylvania, New Jersey, and New York. Captain Teach remained at Bath Town, but as his gold supply dwindled, the temptation to return to piracy rose strongly within him.

Before winter's end Blackbeard was back again at his old trade with some of his favorite henchmen.

The pirates gradually worked their way southward from Bath Town capturing and plundering every vessel they met. It was a free and easy life and Teach felt more at home on the quarter deck of the *Queen Anne's Revenge* than he ever did cooped up in a house on the beach. Seeking relaxation from their arduous work of pyrating, the pirate throng made sail for Turneffe — that wicked, lawless, pirate haven off the coast of Guatemala.

While making Turneffe their temporary headquarters, the pirates made frequent forays into nearby waters to keep their hand in pyrating, to augment their supply of gold, and to help pass the time during their sojourn. Lieutenant Richards aboard the *Revenge* captured four merchant ships. Three of them belonging to Jonathan Bernard of Jamaica were released after all items of value had been confiscated. After ransacking the fourth sloop, they set her afire to teach her master, Captain James, a costly lesson. The fate of a captured vessel often hung on the statements of the crew concerning their treatment by the Captain. If the crew agreed that the captain treated them satisfactorily, the pirates frequently let the vessel go; if not, she was destroyed by burning.

One day during their layover at Turneffe a lookout reported a vessel approaching the harbor. Lieutenant Richards slipped the anchor cable of the *Revenge,* raised the skull and crossbones flag, and ran out to meet the incoming sloop. Immediately the sloop struck her colors, dropped sail, and hove to near the stern of the *Queen Anne's Revenge.*

The sloop proved to be the *Adventure* bound from Jamaica under command of Captain David Harriott. Blackbeard ordered the captain and crew aboard the pirate flagship. It was customary in those days for pirates to invite or even force captured crewmen to join them. This was one way pirate chiefs replenished their crews. Sometimes the captives felt they could improve their lot by joining the pirates. This seemed to be true in the case of Captain Harriott because he and some of his men joined Teach's company of pirates. Captain Harriott must have had some pirate blood in his veins for he remained a pirate until he was killed when Bonnet was captured in the fall of 1718. Israel Hands, Sailing Master of the flagship, was sent with a hand-picked crew to man the *Adventure.*

On March 28, 1718 while cruising about 40 miles northwest of the Cape of Honduras, the *Revenge* came upon the *Protestant Caesar.* This was a vessel of 400 tons carrying 26 guns and a crew of 50 men. She was under the command of Captain William Wyer. Apparently Wyer recognized the approaching sloop as a pirate ship for he put his vessel in fighting readiness.

About nine o'clock that night the *Revenge* caught up with the *Protestant Caesar.* She fired several cannon into the stern of the larger ship together with a volley of small arms fire. Captain Wyer responded by firing two of his stern chase guns and some small shot. He disregarded Lieutenant Richard's threat that if more guns were fired, the pirates would give no quarter. The firing continued until about midnight when the *Revenge* dropped astern. It seems plausible to assume that since the *Revenge* was unable to take the *Protestant Caesar*, she hurried from the scene of battle to get help from the 40-gun pirate flagship.

Back at Turneffe Blackbeard was infuriated when Lieutenant Richards reported that the *Protestant Caesar* had eluded him. The pirate captain was enraged at losing a rich prize, but of more importance, he was furious lest Captain Wyer boast later that he had bested one of Blackbeard's pirate vessels in battle.

Thus it was that the pirate fleet weighed anchor and sailed toward the Bay of Honduras. On the way they took the sloop, *Land of Promise*, commanded by Captain Thomas Newton. Blackbeard told Captain Newton that he was bound for the bay to burn the *Protestant Caesar* such action being necessary to prevent the captain from bragging on his return to New England that he had beaten a pirate.

On the morning of April 8 the fleet of four pirate vessels (one of these was the *Land of Promise)* bore down on the *Protestant Caesar* which was anchored in the bay still loading a supply of logwood. It was abundantly clear to Captain Wyer that the incoming vessels were pirates. Both the *Queen Anne's Revenge* and the *Revenge* sported Black Flags and Death's Heads while the smaller sloops flew Bloody Flags. Hastily summoning his officers and men on deck, Captain Wyer asked if they would stand by him and defend the ship. They answered that if the attackers were Spaniards, they would fight to the death, but, if pirates, they would not fight at all. Immediately Captain Wyer dispatched his Second Mate in the pinnace to ascertain exactly who these pirates might be. The mate soon returned with the depressing news that the pirates were commanded by none other than Blackbeard himself. He also reported that one of the sloops was the very same one that had engaged the *Protestant Caesar* on March 28. Having no belly for a fight with four pirate vessels carrying 50 guns and manned by 300 or more cutthroats, the Captain, Officers, and men deserted the *Protestant Caesar* by going ashore in the long boats. Knowing pirates as they did, they well knew they would be slaughtered after that running battle of a few days ago.

Three days later Captain Teach sent word ashore to Captain Wyer that he would do him no harm if he came aboard the pirate flagship. Captain Wyer boarded the *Queen Anne's Revenge* and spoke with the pirate chieftain. Blackbeard told Wyer he had been wise to surrender because the *Revenge's* crew certainly would have murdered him and all his officers and crew for fighting with them. Also, he said he would have to burn the *Protestant Caesar* because she was out of Boston where some pirate friends had been hanged recently.

The next day Teach sent his Quarter Master, William Howard, with eight crewmen to burn the *Protestant Caesar.* They set her afire and burned her to the waterline, that is, after first stripping her of all valuable cargo.

Blackbeard then allowed Captain Wyer to take passage with Captain Newton aboard the *Land of Promise;* they arrived in Boston on May 31, 1718 and immediately spread the word of the sacking and burning of Wyer's ship.

By mid-May 1718 Blackbeard and his pirate fleet had worked their way northward to the bar outside Charles Town where they remained for five or six days. Teach knew this was a good hunting area because of the heavy ship traffic passing through that busy, thriving port. Captain Teach had promoted himself to the rank of Commodore now being in command of four vessels with a pirate crew of from 300 to 400 men. The pirate fleet consisted of the *Queen Anne's Revenge* under Teach, the *Revenge* commanded by Richards, the *Adventure* in charge of Israel Hands, and a tender which served the three fighting ships.

The first thing the pirates did upon arriving at the Charles Town bar was to show their Bloody Flags to the town and capture the pilot boat. Then they lay in wait for their prey. In quick succession Blackbeard seized the *Crowley* and a small ship commanded by Captain Craigh as both crossed the bar headed for London. The *Arthamethia* under Captain Danford inbound from London also fell to the pirates as did the *William* from Weymouth under Captain Hewes. In short, Teach and his men captured every inbound and outbound vessel and in so doing completely paralyzed all shipping at Charles Town. At this time eight other ships lay in the harbor ready to weigh anchor for their respective ports of call, but their captains were afraid to venture across the bar to certain capture by the pirate fleet.

While each seized vessel was being systematically ravaged by the pirates, all the passengers were held prisoner in the ship's hold. In general pirates were a blood-thirsty lot who would not hesitate to kill or maim a prisoner upon the slightest provocation. But, they were more interested in loot — the gold, silver, or jewels which a captive possessed — than in killing or torturing him.

It was the Quarter Master's job aboard a pirate ship to interrogate all prisoners and it was soon discovered that an important personage of the day had been captured. The celebrity was Samuel

Wragg, a member of the Council of the Carolina Province, whose pocketbook yielded some 1500 pounds in cash to the pirate treasury. Since the prisoners had already been relieved of all valuables on their person, except their clothing, the only thing left to do now was to ransom them for whatever they might bring.

For some unknown reason Blackbeard chose to demand not gold, silver, or jewels, but drugs and medicines in exchange for his prisoners. Having reached this decision, he ordered the Ship's Surgeon to prepare a list of needed medicines. No one knows the true story, but some writers feel that the great Blackbeard was a drug addict and for personal reasons demanded drugs, especially laudanum, in return for the prisoners.

The ransom terms were simple. Either the Governor would immediately furnish the chest of medicine and guarantee the pirate ransom party safe conduct to their ships or the pirates "would murder all their Prisoners, send their heads to the Governor, and set the Ships they had taken on Fire" (1: p. 23). Further, the pirates "threatened to come over the Barr for to Burn the Ships that lay before the Towne and to Beat it about our Ears" (2: p. 74).

The ransom party was in charge of Lieutenant Richards accompanied by Israel Hands and other crew members. One of the prisoners, Mr. Marks, was selected to present the pirates' demands to the

33

Governor. Teach gave them two days in which to complete their mission; after that, he would behead all prisoners.

Two days passed and the ransom party had not returned. Believing his men were either captured or killed by town authorities, Blackbeard ordered the prisoners to prepare themselves for death. They pleaded for one more day of grace. Meanwhile the ransom party sent word that their boat had capsized while crossing the bar which had delayed their arrival in Charles Town. Teach agreed to wait one more day.

The day of grace passed and with it Blackbeard's patience; his terrible temper exploded and he threatened to kill the prisoners immediately. Once more the captives begged for a stay of execution. If the party did not return soon, they promised to guide the pirate fleet over the bar and to aid the pirates in attacking the ships in the harbor and the town itself. Teach paused, after all, he thought, dead prisoners were good to nobody; they could not be turned to a pirate's profit. Persuaded by the prisoners' pleas for mercy, Blackbeard agreed to wait still longer.

The Carolina province had just emerged from a long, costly war with the Indians and was short of men, money, and supplies. The province was in no condition to repel invaders of any kind be they Indians, pirates, or Spaniards from Florida. There were no guns available to protect the harbor nor to arm any of the merchant ships anchored there. There was not a single man-of-war of his Majesty's Royal Navy anywhere within a week's voyage. Furthermore the town had recently been visited by another notorious pirate, Captain Vane, a colleague of Teach's. Vane had given the town a good fright which they had not yet time to forget. Now the entire population was terrorized by Blackbeard's arrival. The men, women, and children of Charles Town were overcome with paralyzing fright. This terror was heightened by a sickening realization that they could do nothing to save themselves.

Upon receiving the pirates' demands, Governor Johnson immediately convened his Council to lay the matter before them. Meanwhile the pirates in the ransom party walked the streets of Charles Town openly and roused the awe-stricken citizenry to near panic. The Council reached a decision quickly; they well knew that Teach was an unpredictable rouge, ruffian, and scoundrel. Who could tell when his uncontrollable temper might erupt resulting in the execution of their friends, the burning of their ships, and the sacking of their town? A chest was immediately filled with medicines and delivered to the ransom party. There was no doubt in the minds of the Governor and the Council that Blackbeard would implement his ultimatum if his demands were not met promptly.

Apparently Captain Teach was satisfied with the medicine chest because he kept his word and released the prisoners — after stripping them of most of their clothing. The captives were set ashore in a near-naked condition at some distance from the town, but they were so glad to escape with their lives that they did not complain of the additional hardships they endured before finally reaching Charles Town.

Blackbeard next turned his attention to the eight or nine ships he had taken during his stay off Charles Town. After removing all provisions needed for his fleet, he destroyed the remainder. Then he permitted his men to despoil the ships "for the pure Mischief Sake and to keep their Hands in."

Having accomplished all the deviltry, destruction, and havoc they could under the circumstances, Teach and his pirate brood now headed northward toward North Carolina. Leading the way was the mighty Blackbeard, the fiercest pirate of all, in his flagship, the *Queen Anne's Revenge*.

Like other pirate leaders, Blackbeard found it necessary to keep his crew busy all the time. Unless they were stalking prey, plundering ships, and robbing prisoners, the pirates tended to grow restless and ill tempered. Johnson reports an incident from Blackbeard's ship's log and written in his own hand:

"Such a Day, Rum all out: — Our Company somewhat sober: A damn'd Confusion amongst us! — Rogues a plotting; great Talk of Separation. — So I look'd sharp for a Prize; such a Day took one, with a great deal of Liquor on Board, so kept the Company hot, damned hot, then all Things went well again" (1: p. 34).

Somewhere off the Carolina coast the pirate fleet seized a brigantine from Bristol. She was bound from Angola and carried 86 negroes for the slave trade. Teach inspected the lot and kept 14 of the best negroes. Strong hands were always needed aboard a fleet such as he now had. Besides, negroes could always be converted into cash when they got to port. Good blacks like these would bring fancy prices — a fact which pleased the corsair chief no end.

The pirates also captured a ship from Boston whose cargo was thoroughly looted. It is not known why Blackbeard chose not to destroy either the brigantine or the other vessel. Instead, he allowed them to limp into Charles Town harbor where on June 12, 1718 they reported Teach's latest piratical atrocities to the authorities.

On the long sail to his old haunts in North Carolina, Blackbeard began to think about disbanding his pirate fleet. He may have had the same feeling once expressed by Henry Morgan: "The fewer we are, the better shares we shall have in the spoils.'' Teach decided to keep all the pirate loot for himself and a few favorite cronies and to get rid of the rest of his crew. As he cruised northward along the Carolina coast, the pirate chieftain completed his diabolic scheme.

On the pretense of careening his vessel at Topsail Inlet near Fishtown (now Beaufort, North Carolina), Blackbeard purposely ran his flagship aground. Pretending this to be an accident, he signaled Israel Hands, who knew of his chief's plan, to pull him off the shoal with the *Adventure*. While pretending to do so, Hands purposely ran the *Adventure* onto the shore and lost her. It was all part of Teach's master plan.

With his two ships aground in Topsail Inlet, Blackbeard suddenly returned Major Stede Bonnet to his former position as Captain of his own ship, the *Revenge*. Unable to comprehend this sudden change in his fortune, but not stopping to question it, Bonnet sailed off to Bath Town.

With Bonnet out of the way, Captain Teach took the sloop which had served as tender to the pirate fleet, loaded it to the gunwales with all the loot she could hold, and sailed away with the rest of the crew. A few miles outside of Topsail Inlet, Blackbeard marooned 17 of his crew on a tiny, sandy island. It was his clear intention that the men should perish because the island was uninhabited; there was no food there nor any materials to build any kind of boat.

Teach's plan had worked perfectly! In one quick stroke he had reduced his fighting force from four ships to one and his pirate band from some 300 men to 23. More importantly, he had all the treasure. Indeed Morgan was right: "The fewer we are, the better shares we shall have in the spoils."

Arriving at Bath Town, Bonnet surrendered to Governor Eden and received a certificate from his Excellency under the terms of the King's Proclamation. About this same time war had broken out between the Triple Alliance and Spain, so Bonnet got clearance to proceed to St. Thomas with the declared intention of seeking a letter of marque to privateer against the Spaniards. However, he had no immediate intention of doing this and, instead, headed back to Topsail Inlet.

While Teach was enroute to Bath Town, Bonnet was returning to Topsail Inlet and Fishtown. Stede Bonnet was both astonished and furious to find Blackbeard gone — with all the treasure! Two of the marooned men had escaped from their island prison and had reached Fishtown. They told Bonnet of the marooning, whereupon he rescued the rest of the pirates from the island.

Aboard the *Revenge* Bonnet informed the crew that he planned to take a privateer's commission against the Spaniards. He urged all hands to join him and they consented. But, just as the *Revenge* was being readied for sea, a market boat selling apples and cider to ships in the harbor brought word that Blackbeard lay at Ocacock Inlet with only 18 to 20 hands aboard.

Major Stede Bonnet had long endured a deep and burning hatred for Blackbeard not only for the way he had been treated those many months while virtually a prisoner aboard the pirate flagship, but for the way Teach recently tricked him and the others by making off with all the booty. Bonnet set sail immediately for Ocacock in hot pursuit of Blackbeard, but he arrived too late; the pirate chief had already left for parts unknown. After cruising around for four days, but unable to spot Blackbeard's sloop anywhere, Bonnet headed out to sea bound not for St. Thomas, but for Virginia. It is not known why he changed his plans so abruptly. Perhaps he never intended to privateer against the Spaniards or he may have decided to become a privateer after first lining his pockets with more pirate gold.

Shortly afterwards Blackbeard returned to Bath Town and surrendered again to Governor Eden. In due time Captain Teach's request for mercy reached the attention of King George I and an official pardon was issued. The pardon never reached Blackbeard; it arrived at Bath Town about a month after he perished in battle.

After surrendering to the King, Blackbeard appeared willing to lead a reformed life. However, this was merely a period in which the pirate king marked time. He took advantage of this opportunity to develop further his understandings with Governor Eden and Tobias Knight. It is quite unlikely, however, that he ever gave serious thought to abandoning his trade.

An early favor which Governor Eden granted Blackbeard was to give him official right to a vessel which had been captured earlier when he was pyrating in the *Queen Anne's Revenge.* This was accomplished by the simple expediency of holding a Court of Vice Admiralty at Bath Town and condemning the vessel as a privateer's prize taken from the Spaniards. However, at the time of the seizure, England and Spain were at peace; Teach never held a

Figure 5

Pistol used by Blackbeard.

letter of marque authorizing him to privateer; and the captured ship belonged to English merchants!

About this time Blackbeard married again. This time he chose Mary Ormond, a 16-year-old girl from Bath Town who was the daughter of Wyat Ormond, owner of a nearby plantation. It is said that the ceremony was attended by Governor Eden — some say the ceremony was performed by the Governor himself. Rumor had it that Mary was Blackbeard's fourteenth wife. Behind his back folks gossiped that at least 12 of Blackbeard's wives were still living scattered along his wake from the Lesser Antilles (Trinidad) to the New England coast. It was even whispered that he had a wife and a son living in London.

To all intents and purposes Blackbeard, the scourge of the Caribbean, settled down to the comfortable life of a Carolina planter. He built a home near Bath Town on Plum Point facing Old Town Creek (now Bath Creek). Just across the creek, but facing the Pamticoe River was Knight's Landing, the home of Tobias Knight, Secretary of North Carolina and right-hand man of Governor Eden.

Teach whiled away the next few months at his Plum Point home and visited with some of the plantation owners along the Pamticoe River. He boasted that he could sup with any planter he chose. While he was cordially received by many of these planters, it is not known if their reception of him was due to a genuinely sincere expression of friendship or to a deadly fear of reprisal if they offended him.

It was acknowledged that Blackbeard was a ladies man. The allegation that he had 14 wives, with or without the benefits of matrimony tends to support this statement. Further, Blackbeard often took undue liberties with the wives and daughters of certain plantation owners who pretended not to notice these social infractions lest they provoke his wrath.

Sometimes the ex-pirate chieftain cruised along the Pamticoe River, the Pamticoe Sound, and adjacent waters, but his favorite mooring spot had always been in Ocacock Inlet in a channel called Teach's Hole. Trading and stealing were still the order of the day. If he were in good humor, Blackbeard might give presents and gifts to the ships' masters for the stores and provisions he took from them. At other times, as his mood changed, he would rob them of what he wanted without recompense knowing full well that they could do nothing about it.

During the summer of 1718 Blackbeard was known to be in Philadelphia. His specific purpose in being there is lost forever in the dimness of Time. The city was well known to pirates as a good place for disposing of illicit goods. Philadelphia merchants were willing to disregard the source of their purchase so long as these could be obtained at bargain prices. Perhaps Teach was in town on such business. Or it may be that he journeyed there to have a fashionable city tailor make several suits of fine clothing for him. At any rate he is known to have swaggered up and down the streets publicly. In fact, these public appearances so annoyed Governor Keith that on August 11 he issued a warrant for Blackbeard's arrest. Forewarned of the Governor's warrant, Captain Teach left town before being apprehended. His informant remains unnamed; perhaps it was a pirate confederate or a Quaker merchant friend. Quakers were well known throughout the provinces for their mild stand against smugglers and pirates. Some Quakers even helped pirates escape from jail!

A few weeks later Blackbeard was cruising near the Bahamas in his sloop, the *Adventure*. In these waters he took two or three English vessels but relieved them only of what food and provisions he needed. On August 22 just east of Bermuda he captured two French vessels homebound from Martinique. One ship was sailing light, but the other was heavily laden with sugar and cocoa. Teach ransacked the vessel which was lightly loaded and then ordered aboard her the captains, officers, and crew from both vessels. Next he set his prize crew on the vessel with the cocoa and sugar cargo and ordered that she be sailed to Ocacock Inlet where she arrived on September 13. If Captain Teach could have peered into the future at this moment, he would have let both these vessels pass unmolested because their capture marked the beginning of his end.

The next day (September 14, 1718) Blackbeard left his anchorage at Teach's Hole near the inlet in a large periangor with a crew of four negroes. The pirate leader's periangor was a large, flat-bottomed boat about 30 feet long with a beam of five and one-half feet and which could carry 20 or more tons. Each end was decked over, but the mid-section was open. His pirate crew could either row or sail the craft by using the schooner-like sails on the two masts which could be struck. Blackbeard found this type of craft especially useful in navigating shoal waters because it used leeboards instead of a keel. It was ideal for his present voyage to Knight's Landing at Bath Town which lay some 53 miles across the Pamticoe Sound and up the Pamticoe River.

Blackbeard was hand-carrying a present to Tobias Knight selected from the loot taken from the French ships. His gift consisted of several kegs of sweet meats, some loaf sugar, a bag of chocolates, and some other boxes whose contents remain unknown. His real purpose in visiting the Secretary of the Province was to complete the arrangements for disposing of the rest of the captured cargo. Arriving at Knight's Landing about midnight, Teach instructed the crew to leave one keg of sweet meats in the periangor and to carry the rest of the contraband gift to Knight's house.

Tobias Knight was home that evening, although he was reported to be in ill health. Blackbeard stayed with him until just before dawn and then departed. It was agreed that the Secretary would prepare the proper papers so that the French vessel at Ocacock would be condemned as a wreck abandoned at sea.

About three miles downriver from Knight's Place was Chester's Landing which marked the home of John Chester. Lying offshore near this point was a periangor carrying William Bell, a Corratuck merchant, his son, and an Indian. When Teach spied this vessel, he ordered his crew to row toward her. As his periangor scraped alongside the other, Blackbeard leaped into Bell's craft. Pointing his sword at Bell's throat, Blackbeard growled, "Damnation seize me, I will kill ye now if ye do not tell me truly where the money is."

Half-frightened out of his wits, but still maintaining a steady composure, Bell responded, "Who be ye and from whence do ye come?"

"I come from hell," roared Teach, "and I will carry ye there presently." With that he began striking Bell with the flat of his sword and in so doing snapped off the blade of the weapon about nine inches from the point. Never dreaming that he was struggling with the terrible Blackbeard, Bell grappled with his assailant until some of the other pirates sprang into the periangor and subdued Bell, the boy, and the Indian.

The pirates now maneuvered Bell's periangor into the middle of the river where they rifled her. This night their loot consisted of 66 pounds in cash, a piece of crape material 58 yards long, a box of pipes, half a barrel of brandy, and some miscellaneous items. One of the latter was a beautiful silver chalice — ''a silver cup of remarkable fashion.'' This cup was later found among Blackbeard's effects in the cabin of his ship following the battle in which he was killed.

After stripping their victims and the periangor of any remaining articles of value, the pirates tossed away Bell's sails and oars. They continued their way down river, across the Pamticoe Sound, and back to Ocacock Inlet.

Several hours later William Bell reached shore and hurried at once to the Governor to complain of the robbery. Governor Eden referred him to Tobias Knight who was also the Chief Justice of the Province.

Upon hearing Bell's story, Knight issued the customary warrant or Hue and Cry. Bell described the periangor and the men who had robbed him. For some strange reason Bell apparently did not realize that he had been attacked by Blackbeard, the fiercest pirate of all. Bell stated that he had seen the pirate craft sail upriver earlier in the evening toward Knight's Landing or Bath Town. Tobias Knight seemed undisturbed by this information and made no comment whatever. He did not volunteer information that the periangor had stopped at his landing nor did he associate Teach's name with this incident.

Blackbeard and his four henchmen reached the island of Ocacock sometime during the daylight hours of September 15, 1718. Pursuant to his arrangements with Tobias Knight, Captain Teach soon returned to Bath Town to confer with his Excellency, Governor Eden, where he signed an affidavit that he had found the French ship on the high seas without a single soul on board. Once again the Governor convened a Court of Vice Admiralty. This time the court declared the vessel to be a wreck at sea without men or papers and so condemned both the ship and its cargo. For his share in these proceedings, Governor Eden was to receive 60 hogsheads of sugar with 20 hogsheads for Secretary Knight.

Teach was shrewd enough to realize that so long as the French ship remained afloat, she constituted a threat to all concerned. He knew that sooner or later the Frenchman would be recognized and this could spell trouble for him and his governmental accomplices. Accordingly he petitioned Governor Eden for permission to destroy the ship by fire on the pretense that she was leaky and her sinking would certainly block the Ocacock Inlet where she was anchored. Apparently this request made sense to the Governor for he granted it immediately. Blackbeard and his men towed the doomed ship into deeper waters of the Pamticoe and burned her to the waterline. As the keel and bottom timbers of the vessel sank beneath the waters, they carried their secret with them.

Blackbeard continued his petty larceny of all vessels that frequented the waters of the Pamticoe. He simply took by force whatever he needed from traders, merchants, and plantation owners. Mere mention of the name, *Blackbeard*, paralyzed the speech and actions of his victims. They quivered and shook in fear as this merciless brute robbed them and thought themselves fortunate indeed to escape with their lives.

One day matters came to a head. The tempers of the traders, merchants, ships' captains, and especially the plantation owners in the Pamticoe Sound area reached the saturation point. They had endured more than enough of Blackbeard's pillaging, robbing, and plundering not to mention his indecent treatment of their wives and daughters. A group of these men met secretly. They realized that it would be a waste of time to seek help from Governor Eden for it was common gossip that he and his Secretary were in some unsavoury way involved with the pirate chieftain. Everyone knew that Captain Teach delighted in bullying Governor Eden publicly, not for any particular gain, but just for the sheer enjoyment of doing it! The pirate was a monster who was ruining their trade, imperiling their lives, and tarnishing the reputations of their wives and daughters.

Legally the problem of extirpating Blackbeard and breaking up his pirate band rightfully belonged to Governor Eden, yet obviously he had no intention of doing anything about Teach. So the planters and traders sent a delegation in great secrecy to their neighboring state, Virginia, to request the help of Governor Spotswood whose firm stand against piracy was well known.

Upon their arrival in Williamsburg, the delegation lost no time in acquainting Governor Spotswood with their grievances against Blackbeard and his ruffians. It was not the first time that the Governor had heard such complaints for he was well informed of the piratical activities in the nearby province. The Governor was told that the situation was rapidly deteriorating. He was reminded of Blackbeard's insufferable conduct with the planter's wives and their marriageable-age daughters. He was informed of Teach's piracies in open disregard for the amnesty granted him in accordance with the King's proclamation. He was shown a sworn affidavit by one of the inhabitants of the province that characterized Teach's insolent behavior and showed how insensible he was of the clemency he had been accorded.

Actually the Governor had first-hand knowledge of some of Blackbeard's most recent piracies. It was just a few months past, in July 1718 to be exact, that William Howard, ex-Quarter Master of the *Queen Anne's Revenge,* had been apprehended in Virginia for trying to enlist some seamen to go a-pyrating. The investigation revealed that Howard had been engaged in piracy after January 5, 1718 (the expiration date of the King's Proclamation) and in so doing had forfeited his pardon. Howard was tried without jury by the Court of Admiralty, found guilty, and was presently in jail pending execution. The Governor recalled that at Howard's trial it was revealed that Blackbeard had taken nearly 20 vessels since January 5 which date was after surrendering to Governor Eden and taking the King's pardon. Yes, Governor Spotswood was well informed about the exploits of the pirate chief, Blackbeard, and his cutthroat band.

The Governor's ire reached a climax when the Carolina delegation played their ace card. They told Governor Spotswood that in mid-September Blackbeard had brought to Ocacock a French vessel laden with sugar, sweetmeats, cotton, and cocoa, but without men or papers. Some of the ship's cargo had already been delivered to Tobias Knight and was believed to be hidden under fodder in his barn. They also reported that Governor Eden had granted permission for Teach to burn the ship on the pretext that she might sink and block the Ocacock channel. Governor Spotswood was aware of the ugly rumors that linked Blackbeard's doings with the provincial government in North Carolina, but nothing had ever been proved. This latest episode, however, suggested a direct connection, perhaps even involving Governor Eden himself.

Governor Spotswood now made a fateful decision and one which would haunt him for years to come. He decided that if the government of the Carolina province could not, or worse yet, would not put a stop to Blackbeard, he would intercede and exterminate him. There were numerous Virginians who were in sympathy with the pirates and the Governor could not be sure whom to trust — even in his own Council or in the House of Burgesses. Accordingly he decided to keep his plans secret and take into his confidence only those few persons he needed.

At that time two guardships from his Majesty's Royal Navy were lying in the James River. These were the *Lyme*, a fifth rate, 32-gun man-of-war under the command of Captain Ellis Brand and the *Pearl*, a fourth rate, 42-gun ship under Captain George Gordon. The vessels had been assigned by

King George I to duty posts in Virginia as guard-ships for the protection of the trade against pirates. Perhaps, reasoned Spotswood, these warships could be deployed to seek out, engage, and destroy Black-beard and his pirate lot.

Captains Brand and Gordon were familiar with the nature of Teach's haunts in the innumerable bays, coves, and inlets of the Pamticoe. They advised Spotswood that their frigates drew too much water to pursue the pirate through the shoal waters near Ocacock. Accordingly Spotswood decided to hire at his own expense two smaller sloops to be manned by officers and men from the crews of the *Lyme* and the *Pearl.* Neither vessel carried cannon; they had only small arms. Pilots familiar with North Carolina waters were to be furnished. Robert Maynard, the first Lieutenant of the *Pearl,* was chosen to command the expedition. He was to sail aboard the larger sloop with a hand-picked crew of 32 men. Mr. Hyde, the First Officer of the *Lyme,* was to command the smaller sloop called the *Ranger* with 22 men. Captain Brand was to travel overland to confront provincial authorities in Bath Town whose complicity with Blackbeard was now suspected by Governor Spotswood.

While these preparations were underway, Governor Spotswood met hurriedly with his Council on November 13 (1718) to finalize a proposal to the House of Burgesses which would pay rewards for apprehending pirates. This bill was especially directed against Blackbeard and proposed rewards over and above those offered by the King's Proclamation. Part of the bill read as follows:

''For Capt. Tach the sum of 100 pounds.
  For every other Commander of a Pyrate Sloop or
    vessel the sum of 40 pounds.
  For every Lieutenant, Master, Quarter Master,
    Gunner, Boatswain or Carpenter 20 pounds.
  For every other Inferiour Officer 15 pounds.
  And for every private man 10 pounds.''
(3:pp. 223-224)

On Monday, November 17 the two sloops slipped their anchor cables in great secrecy and sailed down the James River toward Ocacock Inlet where Blackbeard was reported to be at anchor. The five-day journey carried the expedition to the mouth of the mighty Chesapeake Bay from whence they bore southward on coastal waters. They sailed off-shore of the long chain of sand islands guarding the North Carolina coast which are known today as the Outer Banks. Cautiously they slipped between the Cape of Hatteras and its treacherous shoals lying to the South and East. The charts showed a ''good channel about 3 miles off the Cape'' where the water was 3 fathoms at low tide. From here the King's sloops steered West by South to Ocacock Inlet which lay a distance of 30 miles.

Like others in the chain, Ocacock Island was in 1718 and is today nothing more than a narrow strip of sand separating the Atlantic Ocean from the Pamticoe Sound (see Figure 4). Even today the shifting sands and restless waters continually alter the island's contour and acreage, but in 1718 Ocacock was about 3 miles long and 2 miles wide. A reef of sand, barely covered with water, extended along the island on the Sound side; it was about as wide as the island itself. Generally the land was barren and sandy rising but a few feet above the waters surrounding it. There were swamps and marshes on the island. The only vegetation presiding over this tiny spit of land were gaunt live oak, pine, and cedar trees — all wind battered and salt sprayed. Ocacock Island was sparsely inhabited by a few pilots and their families who eked out an existence piloting vessels across the bar and through the channels leading to the Albermarle Sound as well as to the Neuse and Pamticoe Rivers.

The waters of Ocacock Inlet and the Pamticoe Sound were dangerous (and still are!) especially for strangers. In normal weather the shallow water barely conceals endless shoals, sand banks, and bars. In 1718 the channels were unmarked — what charts existed were inaccurate and out-of-date — so vessels spent considerable time in poling off these sand bars. As if this were not enough trouble for ships' captains, the area was subject to frequent squalls. Violent storms arose without warning and vicious winds churned the waters whipping them into huge white-capped waves. Often hapless vessels had no time to gain safe anchorage.

It was Friday afternoon, November 21 when the expedition from Virginia arrived at the mouth of Ocacock Inlet. The passage had seemed long, but it had been an uneventful one and the sloops had arrived without mishap. The voyage was scarcely half finished because the King's men had to vanquish Blackbeard before they could begin the long trek homeward. But, first they had to find him!

The problem immediately facing Lieutenant Maynard was not only to find Captain Teach and his pirates, but to catch them by surprise lest they slip away in the night. The young officer had prevented all craft, both large and small, from entering the inlet ahead of him and thereby carrying intelligence information to Blackbeard. At the same time he had stopped outbound vessels to learn of the pirates' whereabouts. Lieutenant Maynard learned two interesting bits of information: (1) Teach's sloop, the *Adventure,* was in nearby waters and (2) the pirate chief had only 25 men aboard his vessel, but had loudly boasted to passing craft that he had a crew of 40 men.

And so it was that the North Carolina pilots brought the sloops over the bar and through the

Ocacock Inlet without incident. No doubt the lookouts expected momentarily to spy the masts of Blackbeard's sloop silhouetted against the northeastern sky. Although the lookouts probably could not see to the far end of the channel called "Teach's Hole," it was obvious that the pirate was not in his usual lurking place. Blackbeard's favorite mooring spot had long been a "hole" just off Ocacock Inlet. He had frequented this spot so often that in his time

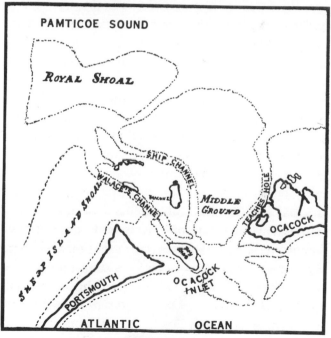

Figure 6
Ocacock Inlet about the time of Teach.

and to this day it is called "Teach's Hole."

As shown in Figure 6, Teach's Hole was not a "hole" or a pool of deep water at all. It was a small, navigable channel lying off the west side of Ocacock Island and provided access through the water-covered sand reef which extended along the Sound side of the island and to which reference was made previously. Teach's channel began off the southwestern corner of the island at the inlet and proceeded in a northeasterly direction roughly paralleling the shoreline of Ocacock. Though narrow in breadth, it was more than four miles long and could be used by ships drawing less than six feet of water.

Teach's Hole was ideally suited for a pirate. His flanks were always protected by the wide shoal on the west and by Ocacock Island on the east. Unless enemies approached simultaneously from both ends of the channel, Blackbeard always had an escape route open. He could flee in either direction down the channel to open water and freedom.

Since Teach was not in his hole, the question facing the King's men was *where could he be?* The Pamticoe Sound is like an inland sea. It is the world's largest sound and is about 100 miles long and ranges between 20 to 30 miles wide. Together with the Albermarle Sound which joins it at the North, it receives the waters of most of the rivers in North Carolina.

Teach could be hidden almost anywhere in the countless coves and bays that dot the coastline of the Sound. He might be somewhere up the Neuse River. He might be anchored along the Pamticoe River anywhere from Bath Town to the Sound — a distance of 25 to 30 miles. If the pirates had received advance warning, it was possible that they had already sailed away.

The sloops "felt" their way as they scouted slowly over the shallow waters of the Sound in the growing dusk. Despite the skill of the pilots, the vessels ran aground constantly. Time after time both craft had to be pulled off sand bars and shoals by the long boat and by men wielding long poles. Lieutenant Maynard had lost count of the number of times they had grounded, but he knew that each delay improved Blackbeard's chances of escape. As the twilight deepened, all eyes strained ahead. Suddenly in the shadows the outlines of two vessels appeared. Maynard was certain that one of these was Blackbeard's ship, the *Adventure!*

It was nearly dark now and with his vessel in strange, shoal waters, Lieutenant Maynard prudently decided not to try to engage the enemy. He signaled Mr. Hyde in the smaller sloop to anchor. Both sloops prepared to pass the night within sight of the pirate vessel.

Captain Teach showed neither surprise nor alarm when he first noted the sloops approaching in the twilight. He was not surprised because he had been forewarned by his friend, Tobias Knight, that trouble was in the wind. While Knight's letter did not directly state that he would be attacked by the King's men, it warned him to be on his guard. Whether or not the Secretary had advance information about Governor Spotswood's plans to destroy Blackbeard may never be known, but his warning letter to Teach was dated November 17 — the same day that the expedition left Virginia bound for Ocacock!

The Secretary had backed up the intimation of danger in his letter by rounding up three of Blackbeard's men which were all the pirates he could find in Bath Town and sent them off in a hurry to find Teach at Ocacock.

Tobias Knight's letter to Blackbeard was as follows:

"November 17, 1718
My ffriend
If this finds you yet in harbour I would have you make the best of your way up as soon as possible your affairs will let you. I have something more to say to you than at present I can write the bearer will tell you the end of our Indian Warr and Ganet can tell you in part what I have to say so referr you in some measure to him.

I really think these three men are heartily sorry at their difference with you and will be very willing to ask your pardon if I may advise be ffriends again, its better than falling out among your selves.

I expect the Governor this night or tomorrow who I believe would be likewise glad to see you before you goe. I have not time to add save my hearty respects to you and am your real ffriend.

And Servant
T. Knight'' (4: pp. 343-344)

Captain Teach was not distressed either by Knight's letter nor by the presence of the two sloops. Several times before he had been warned to be on guard and nothing had ever come of those warnings. As for the sloops, they did not frighten him in the least. He had taken bigger ships than both of them put together. He couldn't even remember half the names of the ships he'd captured; why just since last January there were probably two dozen — maybe more. As a pirate captain he'd won every battle he'd ever been in. He had even made that English man-of-war, the *Scarborough,* run away! If anybody wanted a royal fight anytime, he'd make them wish they'd never heard the name of Blackbeard.

As he stared through the darkening shadows that evening, Teach noted that neither sloop carried cannon; they were too small. That gave him the advantage right away for the *Adventure* boasted eight small cannon. He judged, too, that at most each vessel carried about 25 men; maybe the larger one had a few more. He knew his crew was only 22 strong, but a couple of broadsides from his cannon would even up the odds very quickly.

If Blackbeard made any special battle preparations, they are unrecorded. One thing he did do though was to instruct his faithful black servant, Caesar, to blow up the ship's magazine if the fight went badly on the morrow. Caesar had been with him a long time, so long in fact that Teach often said he'd "bred him up." Caesar could be trusted to obey without question. As soon as the battle was underway, Caesar was to stand by in the powder room with a lighted match ready. If Teach gave the order, Caesar would blow up the ship. If the *Adventure* were to be boarded by the King's men and winning seemed impossible, then Teach, his men, and his ship would be blown to hell, but they would take all the King's men with them!

It is said that Blackbeard stayed up all night drinking in his cabin till dawn with some of his crew and the master of the merchant vessel lying nearby. During the drinking bout one of the pirates asked his Captain, "If ye die on the morrow, does your wife, Mary, know where ye buried the treasure?"

Blackbeard's belly shook with laughter. He

snorted, "Damn ye, my friend, nobody but me and the Devil knows where it's hid — and the longest liver will get it all!"

At first light Lieutenant Maynard roused his crew, hoisted the King's colours, and sent his long boat ahead to sound the water. There was little or no wind, but as the King's sloops moved toward the pirate ship, Blackbeard hailed them saying, "Damn ye for villains, who be ye? And from whence do ye come?"

At once Lieutenant Maynard replied, "Ye can see by our colours that we be not pirates."

"Come aboard me so I can see who ye be," bellowed Blackbeard.

"I cannot spare my long boat," shouted the Lieutenant, "but I will board ye with my sloop."

Blackbeard swore loudly, raised a glass of liquor in salute, and roared, "Damnation seize my soul. I'll give ye no quarter nor take any."

Maynard yelled back, "I expect no quarter nor will give ye any."

Both of the King's sloops were now moving under oars toward the *Adventure*. The men at the oars were exposed because of the low freeboard of the vessels. As the sloops came closer, Blackbeard suddenly fired a broadside of cannon charged with small shot. This barrage inflicted terrible havoc on the King's men. The carnage included 20 men killed or wounded in Maynard's sloop and nine men, including Mr. Hyde, killed aboard the *Ranger*. With their commander lying dead on the deck and no one at the helm, the *Ranger* slowly fell astern and did not return until the battle was nearly over.

Teach now cut his anchor cable and began a running fight while still maintaining continuous fire from his cannon. In a short time the *Adventure* ran aground. Lieutenant Maynard could not reach the stranded vessel because his sloop drew as much water, so he began to lighten his craft by throwing overboard all ballast and by staving in the water casks.

Slowly, ever so slowly, the King's sloop made headway toward the pirate ship which had now turned broadside. Fearing another devastating blast from Blackbeard's cannon, Lieutenant Maynard ordered his men down into the ship's hold. He directed the men to lie down flat, but to keep their pistols and swords ready, and to come up fighting when he gave the signal. Two ladders were readied in the hatchway to speed the men's arrival onto the deck. Before Teach could ready his cannon for another broadside, Maynard's sloop drew alongside the *Adventure*. At this moment the pirates threw a number of grenadoes onto Maynard's deck. These were bottles filled with powder, small shot, and other metallic debris; they had a quick match or fuse in the mouth of the bottle. Upon being lighted the grenadoe had to be thrown quickly because it exploded almost immediately. A grenadoe was a deadly weapon and highly effective in killing or maiming personnel and in causing great confusion, chaos, and disorder among the survivors.

Blackbeard did not know the King's men were in the hold; apparently he assumed they had been blown to bits by the grenadoes. Excitedly he cried, "They're all knocked in the head — let's board them and cut them to pieces." With that he led 14 men onto Maynard's vessel under the smoke cover of the grenadoes.

When Lieutenant Maynard saw the pirates swarming over his gunwales, he screamed to his men, "All hands repel boarders!" With that signal his men sprang from the hold and engaged the pirates in fierce, deadly combat. Figure 7 shows the King's men scrambling from the hold and the desperate duel between Maynard and Blackbeard.

The two leaders sought each other out and attacked first by firing pistols; the Lieutenant's ball struck home, but Blackbeard still lunged forward. Then they fought fiercely with their swords for a few moments, but unluckily the Lieutenant's sword was broken in two by a powerful smash of Blackbeard's cutlass. As Maynard stepped back to cock his pistol, Blackbeard moved in for the kill — fiercely swinging his cutlass. The pirate's blade sought Maynard's throat, but just at that instant Seaman Demelt hacking with his broadsword slashed Teach's face deeply. Blood streamed down the pirate's throat and chest onto the deck. Maynard fired his pistol again, but the brute still stood his ground. The gory battle continued unabated. Lieutenant Maynard and his 12 men fought Blackbeard and his 14 men till the scuppers of the King's ship ran red with blood. Still the slaughter went on. The Lieutenant fired another pistol shot into the pirate chief just as a British Highlander swung wildly with his sword and tore a horrible hole in Blackbeard's throat. Still the mighty Blackbeard kept his feet, roaring at the top of his voice, and fighting on with great fury. Then, as he was cocking his pistol, Blackbeard, the fiercest pirate of all, fell down dead on the bloody deck. He had suffered 25 wounds including five pistol balls in his body before he perished.

By this time eight of Blackbeard's 14 men were either dead, dying, or lay wounded. Some of the others had jumped overboard; they begged for mercy as the King's men fished them out of the water. By now the *Ranger* returned to the fight and her crew assisted in subduing the remaining pirates.

Faithful Caesar, who was waiting below decks to blow up the *Adventure* on Teach's command, waited in vain. The order never came. After the King's men boarded the pirate ship and Caesar learned the battle was ended, he could scarcely be restrained from throwing his lighted match into the ship's magazine. He was clubbed by the King's men and collapsed on the deck where he wept bitterly.

The toll of battle was as follows: Eight of the King's men were killed and 18 were wounded. Of the 54 men on the expedition, 26 or 48% were battle casualties. The pirates suffered 100% casualties. Thirteen pirates, including Blackbeard, were killed

Figure 7
Captain Teach and Lieutenant Maynard fight to the death.

and nine prisoners were taken — all wounded.

Lieutenant Maynard knew he would need proof of Blackbeard's death to collect the rewards posted by the King and the Governor. What better proof could he take back to Virginia than Blackbeard's head? Thereupon the Lieutenant ordered the pirate's head to be severed from his body and hung on the bowsprit of the sloop. The King's men watched in fascination as blood slowly oozed and dripped from the massive head to redden the waters of the Pamticoe.

After attending to the dead and wounded as best they could, Lieutenant Maynard and his 29 able-bodied survivors manned both of the King's sloops and Blackbeard's ship, the *Adventure*. Slowly the King's men sailed across the Sound and up the Pamticoe River to Bath Town to lick their wounds before beginning the long sail home to Virginia.

Blackbeard's death marked the end of piracy in the New World. In one strike the government of Virginia had wiped out the fiercest pirate of all and the most notorious gang of cutthroat pirates ever assembled. About the same time South Carolina made war on two pirate bands operating in her waters. Major Stede Bonnet and 29 of his pirates were hanged near Charles Town on December 10, 1718 — just 19 days after Blackbeard's death. Shortly afterwards Captain Worley and 19 of his men were captured and executed before any of the

Figure 8
The end of the fiercest pirate of all.

wounded pirates could die of their wounds. Thus in one month more than 60 pirates were liquidated. Some piracy continued along coastal waters and especially in the West Indies, but not for long; it never flourished as it had previously. The golden age of piracy in the New World was ended.

The passing of Blackbeard was aptly summarized by his first and most renowned biographer, Captain Charles Johnson, who wrote in 1724:

"Here was an End of that couragious Brute, who might have passed in the World for a Heroe, had he been employed in a good Cause . . ." (1: p. 31)

Blackbeard was a product of the perilous times into which he was born. Illegitimate, uneducated, and untrained in honest ways, he earned his living by the only means he knew — stealing from others. Though his career of crime was brief, Captain Edward Teach achieved infamy as one of the most fearsome sea robbers the world has ever known. More than 250 years have passed since the mighty Blackbeard, the fiercest pirate of all, sailed aboard the *Queen Anne's Revenge*, yet stories of his daring exploits live on today, tomorrow, and perhaps will live on forever.

EPILOGUE

At Bath Town Lieutenant Maynard was joined by Captain Brand of the *Lyme* who had traveled overland to confer with provincial authorities and to seize certain of Blackbeard's goods believed to be stored in the town. These goods, together with several pirates Captain Brand had rounded up in Bath Town, were loaded aboard the King's sloops and preparations were made for the voyage back to Virginia. Final preparations took time and the expedition was still in North Carolina on December 17, 1718. Some days later the three sloops sailed for Virginia waters. Sailing proudly in the vanguard was the pirate ship, *Adventure*, under the command of Lieutenant Maynard with the head of Blackbeard, the fiercest pirate of all, still dangling from the sloop's bowsprit.

It was Tuesday, January 3, 1719 when the *Adventure* reached the Chesapeake Bay. The weather was fair with a slight north to northeast wind stirring. The *Adventure* had no difficulty entering the bay on a broad reach from the mighty

Atlantic Ocean. Turning to larboard (port), the vessel headed in a southwesterly direction where she ran with the wind behind her through the channel and past what is now called Old Point Comfort. With the point on his beam Lieutenant Maynard saluted his commanding officer, Captain Gordon and the *Pearl* with a nine-gun salute. The King's guardship responded in kind with nine guns to the returning warriors. This was a high compliment to the brave Lieutenant and his valiant crew because recently Captain Gordon had been firing but one gun in return to a salute from passing merchantmen.

On January 8 the 15 pirates and the evidence against them were sent by sloop up the James River to Williamsburg. The prisoners were charged with piracy and confined in the public gaol.

A Court of Vice Admiralty was convened on March 12 to hear the charges against the crew of the late Edward Teach, master pirate. The court found 14 of the 15 prisoners guilty of piracy as charged and sentenced them to be hanged. Samuel Odell was the only prisoner found innocent. He had been taken out of the trading sloop moored near the *Adventure* on the night before the battle. Odell must have taken part in the battle because it was reported he received 70 wounds! However, he pleaded he had been forced against his will to serve on the pirate sloop so the court found him not guilty of piracy. Israel Hands, former Sailing Master of the *Queen Anne's*

Revenge, was found guilty. Before he was hanged a ship arrived from England with news that the time limit of his Majesty's pardon had been extended. Hands pleaded his pardon and it was granted.

The remaining convicted pirates of Blackbeard's crew were not so fortunate. All 13 of them were escorted from the public gaol and hanged on 13 trees along Capitol Landing Road in Williamsburg.

REFERENCES

1. *A General History of the Pirates.* Captain Charles Johnson. Edited with a Preface by Philip Gosse. Reprint of third edition originally printed in 1725. The Cayme Press, Stanhope Mews West, Kensington, England. Volume 1. 1925.
2. Letter describing Teach in Charleston harbor, June 13, 1718. British Public Record Office, Volume VII. South Carolina Department of Archives and History, Columbia, S. C.
3. *Journals of the House of Burgesses of Virginia.* 1712-14, 1715, 1720-22, 1723-26. Edited by H. R. McIlwaine, Richmond, Virginia. 1912.
4. *The Colonial Records of North Carolina.* 1713-1718. Volume 2. Edited by William L. Saunders. P. M. Hale, Printer to the State, Raleigh, N. C. 1886.

OTHER READINGS ON PIRACY

Carse, Robert. *The Age of Piracy.* Rinehart & Company, Inc., N. Y. 1957.

Hughson, Shirley Carter. *The Carolina Pirates and Colonial Commerce, 1640-1740.* Johns Hopkins University Studies in History and Political Science. Volume XII, Baltimore, 1894.

Karraker, Cyrus H. *Piracy Was a Business.* Richard R. Smith Publishers, Inc., Rindge, New Hampshire. 1953.

Muller, Edwin. "The End of Blackbeard the Pirate." *Reader's Digest,* Volume 57, No. 342. October 1950, pp. 100-104.

Pringle, Patrick. *Jolly Roger - The Story of the Great Age of Piracy.* W. W. Norton, New York. 1953.

Rankin, Hugh F. *The Pirates of Colonial North Carolina.* State Department of Archives and History, Raleigh, North Carolina. 1965.

Tracy, Don. *Carolina Corsair.* The Dial Press, New York. 1955.

Whipple, A.B.C. *Pirate Rascals of the Spanish Main.* Doubleday & Company, Inc., Garden City, New York. 1957.

Williams, Lloyd Haynes. *Pirates of Colonial Virginia.* The Dietz Press, Publishers, Richmond, Virginia. 1937.

Woodbury, George. *The Great Days of Piracy.* Elek
Books Limited, 14 Great James Street, London,
W.C.i. 1954.

ACKNOWLEDGMENTS

The author wishes to express appreciation to the following reference librarians at East Carolina University who provided valuable assistance in the research underlying this volume: Janet L. Kilpatrick, Martha E. Lapas, Mary Frances Morris, and Marguerite Wiggins.

A special note of thanks is due Tommy Manning, Editor of Literature, Free Will Baptist Press Foundation, Ayden, N. C. whose critique of the manuscript resulted in its great improvement.

Finally, grateful acknowledgment is made to the authors, publishers, agencies, and individuals listed below for the privilege of reproducing selected illustrations in this text:

Figure 1, page 5, from *A General History of the Pirates* by Captain Charles Johnson (1724). Engraving by B. Cole.

Figure 2, page 6, Illustration by Charles Crombe.

Figure 3, pages 20-21, *A Chart of the West Indies* by Herman Moll, Geographer (1710). Courtesy of the North Carolina Room, University of North Carolina, Chapel Hill.

Figure 4, pages 24-25, Moseley's Chart (1733) from *North Carolina in Maps*, (Plate VI) by W. P.

Cumming. Department of Cultural Resources, State of North Carolina, Raleigh, North Carolina.

Figure 5, page 41, State Historic Site, Bath, North Carolina. Photograph by Walter F. Deal.

Figure 6, page 57, "A Description of Occacock Inlet" by Francois X. Martin (1795). Reprinted in the *North Carolina Historical Review*, Volume III (1926), p. 633.

Figure 7, page 67, and Figure 8, page 69, from *Dig for Pirate Treasure* by Robert I. Newsmith. The Devin-Adair Company, One Park Avenue, Old Greenwich, Connecticut.

ABOUT THE COVER

The cover is from a painting, entitled "Blackbeard," by Mildred McMullan Rumley of Washington, North Carolina, in 1955, donated by the artist and now hanging in the Visitors Center at Bath. The color photography is by J. Foster Scott of Manteo, North Carolina. Our thanks to Mrs. John A. Tankard, manager of the Bath State Historic Site, whose interest encouraged the use of this rendering.